Appalachian

Written by
Francie Hall

Illustrated by
Kent Oehm

The Overmountain Press
JOHNSON CITY, TENNESSEE

ISBN 1-57072-087-8
Printed in the United States of America

2 3 4 5 6 7 8 9 0

Dedicated to my children
Miriam, Greg, and Alicia

–FH

Dedicated to my children
Christy and Kevin

–KO

Azalea (Flame Azalea)

A is for *Appalachian Trail*
And the Azaleas along the way.
They add brilliant color
to everyone's day.

Bloodroot

B is for the *Bears*

That roam after a deep sleep

In the soft white snow

so thick and deep.

Christmas Fern

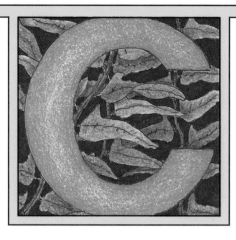

C is for *Christmas trees.*
They are cut and carried far and near
To bring everyone holiday cheer.

Dogwood (Flowering Dogwood)

D is for *Dulcimer.*

Players lightly tap the strings

While the dancers have whirly flings.

Evening Primrose

E is for *Estates*

Of inventors like the "Denim King."

Making blue jeans was

his favorite thing.

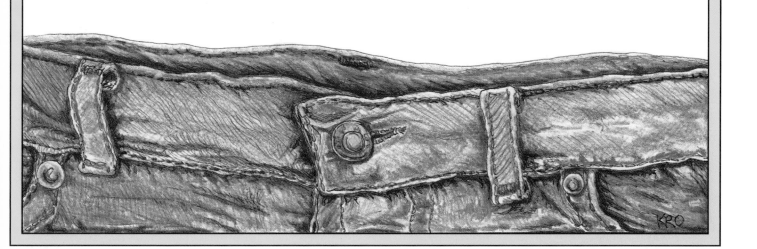

Flowering Raspberry

F is for *Farmer's Market.*
As the hot summer days unfold,
Fresh fruits and flowers
wait to be sold.

Galax & Ginseng (Sang)

G is for *Galax* and *Ginseng*.
Galax is used for decoration.
Ginseng is used for medication.

Hepatica (Liverwort)

H is for *Honeybees*.
In honeycombs they leave
a syrupy treat.
Honey with hot biscuits is
good to eat.

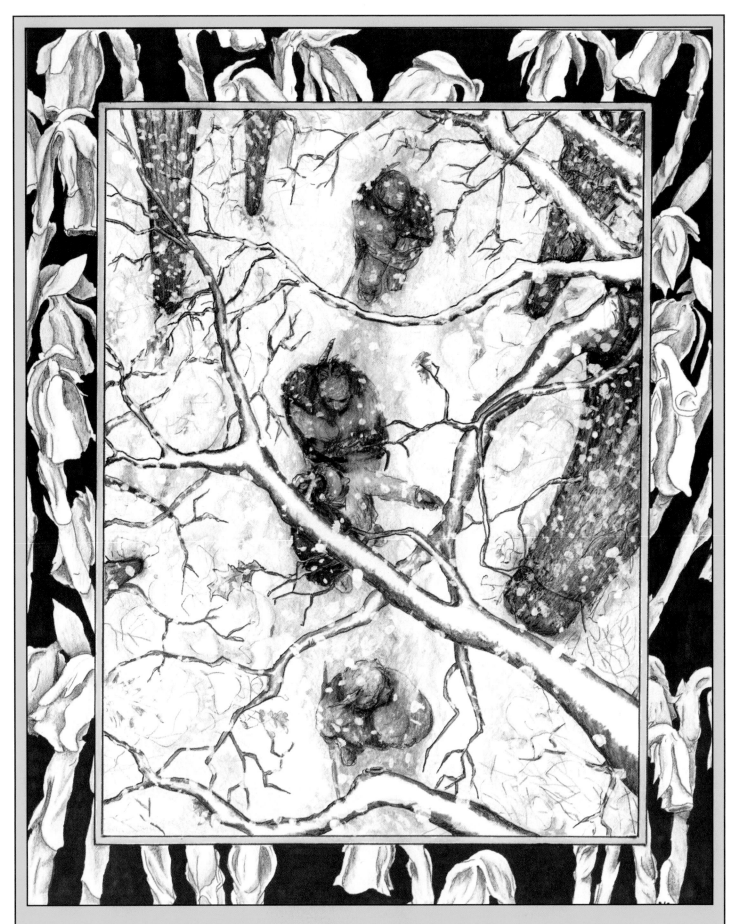

Indian Pipes

I is for *Indians*

Who first lived in our fair lands.

We now call them Native Americans.

Jack in the Pulpit

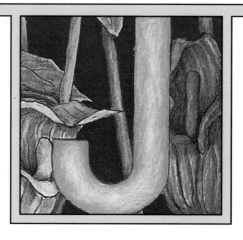

J is for *Jack Tales*.
Once when a mighty North Wind rose,
Jack and his mother nearly froze.

Kalmia (Ivy, Mountain Laurel)

K is for *Kayak,*
Which is a long and narrow boat.
In rivers it will glide and float.

Lily-of-the-Valley

L is for *Log homes* with chimney tops.
They puff gray smoke quietly and still
While nestled calmly on a rolling hill.

Mountain Ash

M is for *Mills*
That grind grain into flour,
Filling several bags every hour.

Necklace Weed (Baneberry)

N is for *National parks and trails.*
They are travelled by mountain bikers
And adventurous alpine hikers.

Obedient Plant

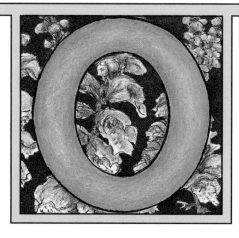

O is for the *Opossum*
Often seen along the road at night.
Her beady eyes stare into the light.

Pale Jewel Weed

P is for *Pottery*

Made from special mountain clays.

They can be dull or have a shiny glaze.

Queen Anne's Lace (Wild Carrot)

Q is for *Quilts*
With patterns colorful and bright.
They keep you warm when
tucked in tight.

Rhododendron

R is for *Rhododendrons*.
Full of blossoms pink and red
A true mountain flower, it is said.

Sneezeweed

S is for *Snow Skiing*.

Whether it's cross-country or downhill,

Here's hoping skiers won't take a spill.

Trillium (Wake Robin)

T is for *Toys* handmade in the Appalachian Mountains that whirl and clack, spin and tap.

Umbrella Tree

U is for *Underground caves*
With stalactites and stalagmites.
Cold and icy-looking,
 they make beautiful sights.

Virginia Creeper

V is for *Virginia Reel.*
To this fast and lively tune
Dancers spin around the room.

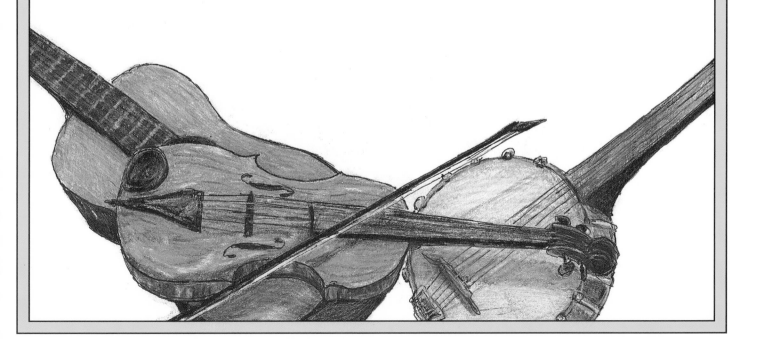

Wood Sorrel

W is for *Wreaths*
Made of evergreen or
dried grapevine
They are often accented
with bows or twine.

Xerophyllum Asphodeloides (Turkey Beard)

X is for *Crossed skis*

Asking for help on the slope.

Then everyone slows down – we hope.

Yellow Lady Slipper

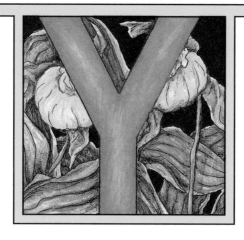

Y is for *"You all."*
It's a way of speaking
To show you care
And have southern hospitality
to share.

Zephyr Lily

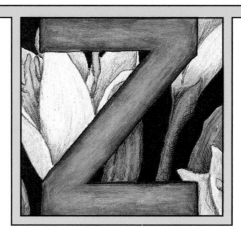

Z is for *Zea mays*.
A plant that grows wild and tall,
Commonly known as corn by all.

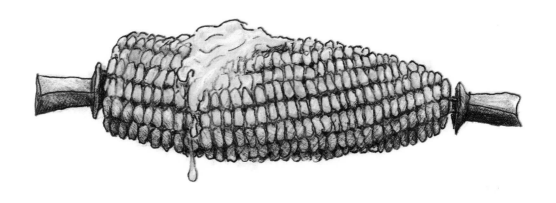

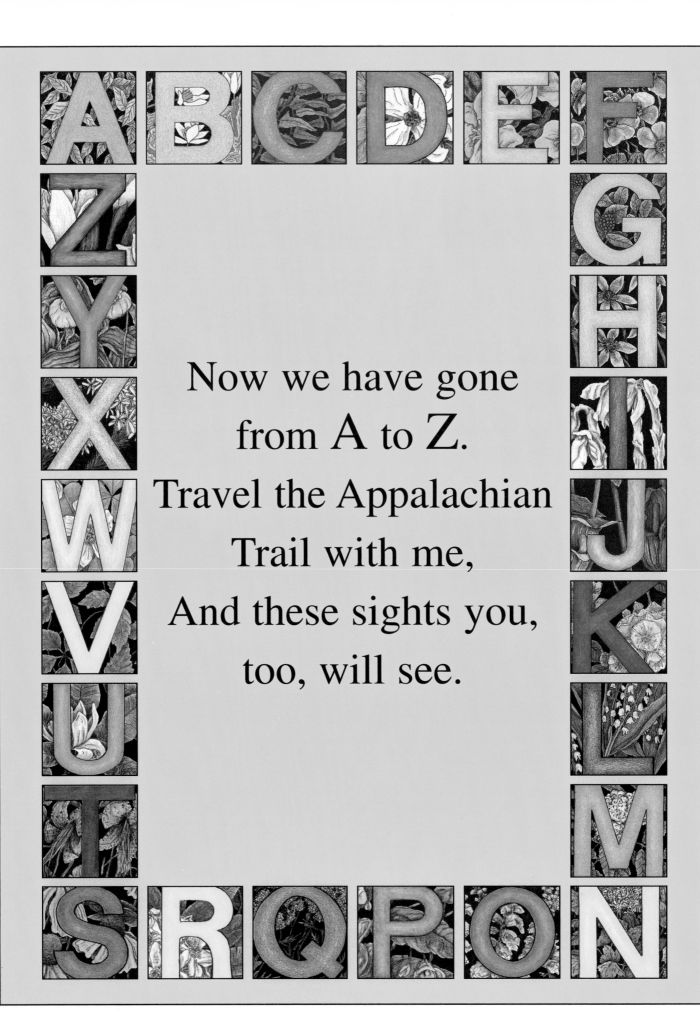

Now we have gone
from A to Z.
Travel the Appalachian
Trail with me,
And these sights you,
too, will see.